STAY OUT OF THE WOODS

STRANGE ENCOUNTERS

VOLUME 2

Compiled and edited by
Tom Lyons

STAY OUT OF THE WOODS:
STRANGE ENCOUNTERS, VOLUME 2

Copyright © 2021 Tom Lyons

All information and opinions expressed
in *Stay Out of the Woods: Strange
Encounters, Volume 2* are based upon
the personal perspectives and
experiences of those who were generous
enough to submit them. Tom Lyons does
not purport the information presented
in this book is based on accurate,
current, or valid scientific knowledge.

Acknowledgments

It's certainly no easy task for people to discuss their encounters with cryptids. I'd like to personally thank the many good people out there who took the time and energy to put their experiences into writing.

To respect those involved, a few of the following names were altered or replaced with "anonymous".

Would you like to see your report in an issue of *Stay Out of the Woods: Strange Encounters*?

If so, all you have to do is type up a summary of your experience and email it to Tom Lyons at:

Living.Among.Bigfoot@gmail.com

Special Offer

If you submit a report and it is accepted, you will receive an exclusive paperback copy signed by Tom shortly after the book is released. If you'd like to participate in that offer, be sure to include your mailing address in the email.

Contents

Report #1

Hi, my name is Lauren, and I faced the most frightening event of my life in the early 90s. Every August, our parents would send my little brother, Jack, and me away to summer camp for a few weeks. Our family lived in Oregon throughout my whole childhood, so there were plenty of options to choose from. I was 12 years old, and that year ended up being my last attending those camps because I refused to go again. I refused to even go to any remote, wooded areas until well into my late twenties. Honestly, I hate thinking about my experience; it's hard for me to talk about it, but I believe we need to get these things off our chests to have any chance of encouraging a more open-minded society. It's the only way we'll ever be able to spread awareness that these things do happen and that cryptids do roam this earth.

During the summer that this happened, a counselor from one of our previous camps decided to start his own venture. My parents really liked the guy. His name was Jacob, and he was one of those people who seemed never to stop smiling. It must have been super easy for him to instill a ton of trust among parents; we all liked him very much. But I think it was because of all that trust that people let it slide how underprepared he was to run his new business. I remember hearing that his family was quite wealthy, so maybe they granted him the capital needed to secure the land but neglected to check that he was abiding by the county guidelines. Who knows?

The location was so isolated that I don't even remember what it was called. I recently asked my parents, and they too have no recollection. I'm not even too sure the area had an official name. Maybe Jacob and a few of his friends drove out into the mountains until they found an unoccupied land near a river. I'm not going to say the exact name of the camp, but I will say that it was something very cheesy. I'll refer to it as

Happy Times Camp, just for the sake of giving it a similar title. The buildings on the property looked like they had been around for a long time but had recently received fresh coats of sky-blue paint. The look of the property led me to believe that it once might've been used for another camp. I had a bit of an off-feeling when we first arrived, but I probably attributed that to the notion of how isolated we were.

That area was beyond beautiful. Aside from a roaring river, it was full of meadows, green hills, and of course, dense woodland. If it weren't for the fact that I was heading into my teenage years, I most definitely would've enjoyed the idea of being dropped off there a lot more.

I'm pretty sure that it was only the first or second night at *Happy Times Camp* that a fellow camper, Clarissa, screamed and woke everyone in our bunkhouse in the middle of the night. She claimed she had rolled over in her bed and saw a pair of glowing eyes staring at all of us from just outside the window. Our counselor, Julie, immediately got out of bed to take a look. She flipped on the lights, making it impossible to see whether anything was looking in from outside. I remember how she didn't even bother to look toward the window since she automatically concluded that Clarissa must've had a nightmare and woke herself up. Another girl, Sammy, complained to me the next day about how she had to listen to Clarissa ramble about the eyes all morning. Allegedly, she kept saying that she didn't want to be at camp anymore, but even her parents dismissed her story of what happened the previous night.

Aside from Clarissa's unrest, the next few days played out normally. There were probably around twenty to thirty kids altogether, and we spent the afternoons playing games like dodgeball, flag football, etc. Early in the trip, the counselors deemed it too unsafe to swim in the nearby section of the river. A lot of kids complained about it, but it was probably the right thing to do. As I said, I'm not so sure Jacob even acquired the appropriate permits to run the camp in the first place; therefore, I can't even imagine how hard the legal system would've gone after him if a child drowned under his supervision.

We had maybe been there for about a week when Jacob announced during breakfast that the counselors had located a calmer, safer section of the river but that we would have to walk a whole mile to get there. Of course, the mile-long walk discouraged a bunch of the lazier kids from wanting to go, and I can't help but wonder if that was part of Jacob's strategy all along. I think the only reason he and his friends went out searching for a calmer part of the river was that they didn't want the parents to hear that there had been no swimming throughout the whole time that their kids were at camp. Indeed, that would be terrible for future business.

Of course, my brother and I insisted on being in the first group to go swimming, and Julie was nice enough to grant us that wish. As our group of about ten people hiked along the river, none of us had a single clue about what more than likely watched us from the other side.

I remember we were sweating profusely by the time we reached a sandy, shallower bend in the river. If my memory is accurate, there was a natural dam that briefly broke the speed of the flow. So it made complete sense why they would've decided that that was the place to take the campers. Ideally, they would have established camp in that area, but it was probably much too wooded and the encompassing terrain too uneven and treacherous.

The depth in that part of the river couldn't have exceeded three feet because I recall walking to the opposite shoreline without swimming. Another kid, Bryan, was already over there, stacking a mound of broken shells. I'm no expert on nature, but they looked like they had once belonged to a species of clam. Whatever they were, it was clear that something had enjoyed an open buffet full of them.

"Lauren, come see this!" Jack later called out from the woods. He walked me maybe ten yards into the forest, where his friend, Brent, found what I at first thought were many piles of manure. I might be completely wrong on this estimation, but I'd guess there were about fifteen of them. Many of them were pressed right up against large trees, making them seem like extensions of the wood rather than separate objects. The more time I spent observing them, the more they began to resemble beehives or hornet's nests, only they were much larger. Each one was maybe a bit below my chest in height. Another interesting thing was how none of these supposed nests appeared to have openings, leading me to wonder how whatever built them got in or out. However, I soon noticed the extensive array of holes in the soil throughout that section of forest.

There was a potent stench among the area, and I'd say it was almost like the smell of decaying meat mixed with a hint of body odor. If it hadn't been for the fact that we could hear the counselors and other campers from where we stood, I suspect the three of us would've been too creeped out to continue examining the area.

A few minutes later, Jack and I headed back toward the river while

Brent stayed behind. He had had a bunch of those small clamshells in the pockets of his bathing suit, and he started using them to design a smiley face on the side of one of the nests. He seemed to think he was very clever for doing so. Then, less than ten minutes later, a sudden shriek caused everyone in and around the river to stop what they were doing and face the trees. Out came Brent, running and crying while holding his bloodied hand in front of him.

"What happened?" Julie screamed as she went running out of the water to meet the little boy at the shore.

"It...it stabbed me," Brent said, visibly in a state of shock.

"What stabbed you?" Julie said just before turning and asking anyone who had it to bring her a dry article of clothing.

"The...it...an elf," Brent continued to stutter.

Julie didn't reply after that because she probably assumed that the kid was confused. In any case, her focus was on wrapping the wound in her towel.

Even though it wasn't a fatal injury, it must've been the most blood I had ever seen up to that point in my life. Aside from that incident, I had probably only encountered a handful of scrapes and bloody noses. Unfortunately, the incident cut our time in the river short, and our group made its way back to camp as quickly as possible.

The camp "nurse" was this tall and skinny guy with long, curly hair and glasses. He was super friendly, but I doubt he was qualified to treat wounds, especially deeper ones like Brent's. So for the rest of that day, nobody got much of a chance to speak to the kid because the counselors decided he needed to take it easy. In some weird way, it felt like they imprisoned him in the bunkhouse, and the following day, I found out why.

While we ate breakfast, my brother told me about his conversation with Brent from the previous night. Something felt very off as soon as I found out that the counselors discouraged the wounded kid from sharing his story with the other campers. According to Jack, Brent claimed that a "little man" crawled up the nest and stabbed his hand while he was designing the smiley face of clamshells. Sure, that story sounded a bit ridiculous, but there *was* something very unusual about those mounds. Then I started to consider the glowing eyes Clarissa claimed to see outside of the girls' bunkhouse. My gut warned me that *something* very unusual lurked around *Happy Times Camp*.

Later that afternoon, I spotted Brent sitting on the bench, reading a book, outside the boys' bunkhouse. Since he was alone, I decided it was an opportunity to see how he was doing and maybe get some direct insight regarding what happened that previous day by the river. I noticed how he looked in all directions as soon as I inquired about the *little man*, clarifying that he had been told not to discuss it with his fellow campers. Something about that rubbed me the wrong way. Even if the poor kid somehow imagined the whole thing and had accidentally jabbed himself with a sharp object, nobody should have the ability to silence him. That just wasn't right. However, as soon as he started talking about it, I knew that he genuinely believed what he saw. It turned out that my brother hadn't misunderstood his friend; everything he mentioned to me that past morning, Brent further elaborated on.

The kid said he had just started creating a face on a second mound when a creature that looked a bit like an elf crawled up it from the other side and sliced his hand. He said that the creature used a very sharp small spear that looked like it was made of wood and rock. Brent said the thing wasn't wearing any clothing and hissed at him as it jabbed his hand. When he screamed, the creature ran back down the mound and then into one of the holes in the ground. Sure, I thought there was still a chance that fear caused him to misjudge what he had encountered, but the look in his eyes indicated that he was by no means attempting to make anything up.

"Lauren, what are you doing?" another counselor, Marietta, called out to me. "Brent needs to rest." Unfortunately, that cut our conversation short, and I had no choice other than to walk away.

I had planned to discuss the whole thing more with Brent whenever I got another opportunity, but frustratingly enough, I learned the very next day that his parents had taken him home. I've always wondered whether Jacob and the other counselors decided it was better to have the boy's parents get him than to risk having all the campers hear about what he saw (regardless of the truth).

The next few days were quite casual, filled with routine activities. The idea of the *little man* began to fade with each new morning; that was until another small group of campers returned from the river, a few of which were crying hysterically. I vividly remember the sudden horrible feeling in my stomach when I got a look at little Chloe's face. Her eyeball was protruding from the socket. One of the counselors kept trying to cup that region of her head, but Chloe kept pushing their hand away. It must've been too painful for her to have anything even remotely near it. It was challenging to wrap my head around what I was looking at, but I just knew that whatever had assaulted Brent had also assaulted this little girl.

More and more campers who hadn't gone to the river continued to gather around the panicked group, determined to learn the origin of the gory accident. That frustrated Jacob and the other counselors, so they commanded the children to head for their assigned bunkhouses. It was the first time I had ever seen Jacob yell at anyone. Until then, I didn't even know it was possible for him to become so agitated. Every other camper seemed to have the same reaction to Jacob's loss of composure, and we did as we were told.

To better suit the grim situation at hand, it soon started to storm while we all awaited an update from inside our bunkhouses. It's almost humorous how mother nature seemed determined to make that afternoon as dark and ominous as possible. Julie eventually entered the bunkhouse with various board games from the common house with the cafeteria. She shushed the first girl to ask how Chloe was doing and looked like she was moments away from pulling her hair out, likely questioning why the hell she ever thought it would be a good idea to work all the way out in the middle of nowhere. That was the first moment where I could tell she was afraid of something but was doing everything in her power to stay calm and in control. The campers seemed to feel Julie's tension and assumed it was best to keep quiet while she went into the bathroom and changed into dry clothes.

The sounds of the storm ramped up while most of the girls in my bunkhouse near-silently dispersed into groups by their selected board games. Eventually, Julie emerged from the bathroom, and it was easy to tell that she had been crying in there. What was she crying about? Everyone continued their calm demeanor while she got settled on the floor near the group playing a game of *Uno*. Thankfully, they all resisted the urge to ask the distressed counselor for news regarding Chloe's condition; nobody wanted to see the tense young woman snap.

The energy in the bunkhouse was very awkward; the girls were making an effort to have fun, but the recent grim occurrence made it too hard to think of anything other than blood. I think it's safe to assume that everyone around me had begun longing for their parents to pick them up.

Our quiet routine continued for maybe half an hour before the storm began to simmer. Julie regularly glanced at one of the windows, each time reevaluating whether she should head out and rendezvous with the other counselors. Eventually, she stood up after finishing her current *Uno* game and told us that she would be back in a few minutes. Of course, the chatter increased in her absence, and the girls openly speculated about Chloe's fate. I remember watching one girl tear up after another girl expressed the possibility of Chloe having died.

After Julie had been gone for nearly half an hour, the talk of potential dark scenarios only worsened, making even more girls desperate to find their way home somehow. Suddenly, our conversations were interrupted by a bunch of shouting coming from the boys' bunkhouse. I could've sworn I heard the words "get away" several times. We all sat there in silence, listening for clues that could explain whatever had just happened. Although the rain was milder by that point, it still drowned out most noise that occurred outside of the bunkhouse.

"Do you think we should go check to make sure they're all okay?" a girl said, disrupting the eerie silence.

"Julie would probably flip out if she found out any of us had gone outside," another girl said.

A girl who was by the window leaned her head to the side, hoping to obtain a view of the boys' bunkhouse, but it proved to be no use. I noticed her gaze quickly turned toward a different direction. "I think I just saw some animals," she said.

"What kind of animals?" someone called out.

"I'm not sure," the girl near the window said. "They were kind of far away, over near wood line. They could've been a pack of coyotes."

Just when things seemed like they couldn't get anymore ghastly, a couple of girls, Lynn and Stephanie, screamed out in horror, causing my heart to nearly leap out of my chest.

It was before I could find out what caused the panic that more girls started screaming.

"Oh my god, what is that?" one girl shouted as she ran over to the wall near the bathroom door. I swiveled my glance in the opposite direction, and when my eyes landed on it, it seemed to take my breath away. There it was: at first glance, it looked like a sizeable four-limbed crab, about the size of a cat, was clinging to the window and looking in at us. It wasn't moving when I first saw it, and it was difficult to know where its beady, seemingly all-black eyes were focused. There was something slightly human-like about the shape of its bald, grey head. Its ears were tiny but protruded from the sides. I still can't make any sense of how it so easily stuck to the window.

Aside from the greyish skin tone, its hands didn't look very different from a human's; however, I'm not sure about the number of extremities. The only reason I mention that is because I've read multiple accounts that claimed this rare species has only three fingers and one thumb on each hand. Anyhow, I thought the most bizarre part about it was how this seemingly solitary creature didn't seem the least bit intimidated by all of us staring at it. Although I couldn't hear it, due to the constant sound of rain, a sudden reshaping of its lips made it look like it was hissing at us. It appeared to have human-like gums, but the teeth were much smaller and more pointed than ours. There was also more space between each tooth than what we have.

I'm not sure how long that strange creature clung to the other side of the glass, but I lost track of it as soon as everyone started screaming when the door burst open. We were all horrified that it was another one of those things making its way into the bunkhouse, but it turned out to be Julie. She was holding a horseshoe, and her hair was smeared against her face. The presence of blood on her legs, along with several gashes, was enough to confirm that something had attacked her. She seemed out of breath, like her struggle to get away had drained her endurance. I found myself wondering if she had actually used the horseshoe as a weapon or if she had quickly grabbed it on her way back inside in case she needed to defend herself again. That whole sequence had to have happened in under ten seconds, but by the time I turned my attention back to the window, the human-like creature was no longer in sight.

"Julie, what happened?" a few girls asked simultaneously.

"I want you all to move to the center of the room," she said. Her voice cracked a bit, reaffirming that she was choked up from tears of terror.

"Right now!" she commanded when a portion of the girls hesitated. It's not like they were trying to disobey her; they were just so frightened by the unfamiliarity of the alarming situation. There were several moments where I decided that I must just be having a deranged nightmare, even going as far as to pinch myself as a strategy to wake myself up. But all those attempts proved to be futile; this was as real as it gets.

"The police are on their way," Julie said as we huddled near the center of the room. I have to admit that sentence was like music to my ears. When you're a child, you have this concept that there's nothing the cops can't handle; therefore, I pretty much felt like we were already safe. Of course, the older you get, the more you learn that police can sometimes feel overwhelmed, no matter how courageous they might be.

"How long until they get here?" asked a girl by the name of Gabby.

Julie opened her mouth to respond but was interrupted by more screams coming from the boys' bunkhouse. They weren't just screaming from fear; some were crying from pain. My heart began beating even faster when I couldn't help but imagine what could happen if a group of those menacing creatures infiltrated our bunkhouse.

As I looked around at the flimsy wooden structure surrounding us, I knew nothing was preventing them from coming in. I wondered if the creatures were hard at work slaughtering the boys and if they'd be headed for us to do the same right after they finished. I would've given anything to have had the power to get my brother out of there, and I did everything in my ability to convince myself that he was still unharmed.

If the best defense we had was Julie and her horseshoe, we were doomed. Frankly, even at my young age, I knew it was a miracle that she survived any threatening situation.

"I don't know what they are," Julie murmured, "but we need to do everything we can to keep them away until help arrives."

There were a handful of occasions where a few girls claimed to have heard footsteps on the roof, but I suppose it could've been the rain changing direction. I don't know how long we stayed huddled together, awaiting any sign of an incoming attack, but I spent a lot of it thinking I was going to die.

For many of the girls around me, tears of fear turned to tears of relief once we heard police walkie-talkies approaching the vicinity. The sounds from multiple radios indicated that at least a few officers were present. Not too long after that, a chopper equipped with a searchlight hovered from above.

I assumed that it would be any moment that we'd hear an officer knock on the door before letting themselves in, but instead, we heard several gunshots. The next thing that we heard was a hair-raising shriek. It didn't sound like it came from a human, nor did it sound like it came from an animal; to my ears, it sounded demonic. We listened to that same type of sequence several times while the helicopter circled from above, eventually choosing a stationary spot closer to the boys' bunkhouse.

Desperate to lighten the mood while we awaited our fate, Julie started singing *The Ants Go Marching*, but, in my opinion, all it did was add to the weirdness of the situation. A few of the girls joined the counselor, but it just sounded creepy.

I couldn't make out exactly what the police officers were shouting to one another, but it seemed to me that they were just as surprised by the little freaks as we were. Can you imagine getting dispatched to a scene where those creatures immediately confront you? It makes me wonder if they had at least been briefed on how things like that exist in the area.

At last, the gunshots stopped, and the long-awaited knock at the door occurred. The officer entered the bunkhouse with his weapon drawn but quickly ascertained that the interior was free of the creatures.

"Everyone alright?" he said just before another older officer entered the bunkhouse. The first officer radioed for paramedics as soon as he laid eyes on Julie—the only one out of our group who had suffered any injuries.

"I'm fine," she said, knowing that the call was for her. "I'll be okay." She focused more on the notion that we had been rescued rather than the lingering pain from her wounds. We were instructed to stay put for probably about twenty more minutes before enough vehicles arrived to transport us out of the area. In the meantime, we packed our stuff while officers came in and out of the bunkhouse.

I glimpsed a couple of ambulances leaving the scene when they escorted us outside. The helicopter resumed circling above us while I wondered which boys and counselors were in the backs of those emergency vehicles. Had anyone died? What if the majority had? They rushed us out of the bunkhouse so quickly we didn't get a chance to look around. The police probably had orders to shelter us from the mayhem.

After that, all I remember is being driven down a winding mountain road in a van, seated between two girls. By that point, it seemed we were all too shaken to cry. They brought us directly to what must've been the cafeteria when we arrived at the police station. When I laid eyes on my brother, Jack, the relief that I felt was perhaps the most powerful sensation I've ever experienced. And even better, he turned out to be unharmed. The staff provided us snacks such as granola bars, apples, and juice boxes while taking down our parents' names and our home phone numbers. I sat next to my brother, somehow knowing it was best to avoid inquiring about his experience, at least for the time being.

I expected to get a better explanation of everything after I eventually got in the car with my parents, but it turned out they were hoping for the same thing. I remember having no idea what to tell them other than that "little people" had attacked the camp. I could tell that they found it very hard to believe my interpretation, and I soon learned that the police said to them that one of the counselors was "involved with some very bad people." Allegedly, these "bad people" had decided to get their retribution at the place they figured he'd be most vulnerable. In other words, the authorities told my parents that it was human criminals who ambushed the camp. I can attest that that was anything but the case. We were invaded by a bunch of that odd-looking creature that had clung to the window and hissed at us, and there's no chance anyone will ever convince me otherwise.

Nobody in my family ever received a proper disclosure on who made it out of *Happy Times Camp* alive, nor did we ever hear from Jacob again. My mom suspected that he left town because he was so embarrassed by what happened, but I've kind of always assumed he probably died. I didn't find out until I started writing this report that my parents received a check a few weeks after the incident, which reimbursed them for the *Happy Times Camp* fees and gave them a bit extra for their troubles. The strangest aspect was that the checks were from a government agency, which hints that they wanted to keep the whole incident on the down-low. To me, that bonus money comes off as a form of bribery, and, hey, I suppose it worked! After I began writing this report, I reached out to the police station that I'm pretty sure was the one involved all those years back. I had hoped that maybe someone would be kind enough to send me any documents that might share some additional details, but as expected, no one ever got back to me.

There's probably no way I'll ever find out exactly what it was that we encountered that night, and I recognize that's something I need to accept. But please bear in mind that there *are* unknown species' of highly dangerous creatures in the woods that very few people will warn you about. So if you love to journey through desolate locations, please always be on the lookout, especially if you have children with you. Stay safe out there!

Report #2

My name is Jim, and I can already feel it will be an interesting experience finally putting my story to paper. For reasons I never thought to be possible, I quickly regretted relocating my family to Ozark, Missouri, from Saint Louis. The last thing I wanted to do was uproot our kids' lives, but I didn't see any other way if I was going to ensure that our new restaurant got up and running and had the best chance of remaining successful. My brother, Gary, had been nagging me since our early twenties about opening a pub and grub together.

There was no hiding the fact that I had grown tired of my career in medical sales, and something finally hit me one day that I should reinvest my savings into something that would make me feel more fulfilled. I needed something that would genuinely excite me when getting out of bed every morning. Even though my brother didn't have the money required to put into the joint, I knew his social skills, work ethic, and determination would be invaluable.

By the time Gary and I had shaken hands on the deal, I had been commuting to Ozark nearly every weekend for half a year. I wanted to be very thorough in picking the suitable building for an alluring business and the right street for my family. It was important to me that the kids would have a safe environment with lots of woods and fewer cars. I wanted to know that they would be able to ride their bikes around the area while only responsible neighbors drove through.

I didn't even tell my wife, Katie, that I wanted us to move out there until a week or two before Gary and I closed a deal on the building we'd use for business. And when I told her, I made sure that I had several attractive home listings ready for her to browse. I felt that both the increase in kitchen space and backyard space would help me convince her that it was the right move. The yard on our chosen property had to be at least eight times the size of what we had in St. Louis. It was perfect for our dog, Oliver, to run around like the mad man that he was. He was a Yellow Laborador, a breed that requires a lot of space to exert all of that energy.

All three of our kids complained about the move until they stepped foot in their new home. I suspect it was the race to conquer the best bedroom that provided a nice little distraction, giving them their first thing to be excited about. Everything about the new house and my new business venture got off to a good start. But I believe it was a couple of weeks after we moved in that Oliver started acting hysterical in the middle of the night. The combination of incessant barking and whimpering would've been loud enough to wake up any crowded neighborhood. The behavior was so unlike anything we had ever witnessed from him. He usually slept on the floor beside one of the kids, but we found him downstairs near one of the doors that led to the backyard. I figured he must've gotten a whiff of either deer or coyotes, so I opened the door, expecting that he wanted to investigate further. I couldn't believe it when he just stood there, looking at me. Never before had he not dashed outside when given an opportunity.

"Go ahead, buddy!" I said, reaffirming that it was okay for him to head out there, but he still didn't budge. Soon, soft whimpering made it seem like he wanted me to close the door.

"What is the matter with you?" I said, concerned for the furriest member of our family. It was after I closed the door and turned around that I felt it for the first time. It was this undeniable feeling that I was being observed, but by who, or *what*? I glanced over my shoulder but couldn't see anything but the darkness and the glare from the stairway light. Oliver was staring in the same direction, but his new demeanor conveyed that perhaps it was unwise for him to have caused a stir in the first place. I gave it a few more seconds before ultimately deciding to brush the feeling aside and head back upstairs.

"C'mon, buddy," I said, and after one more moment of uncertainty, he followed my lead up the steps.

I remember it being a challenge to fall back asleep that night. What was it that had managed to make our dog go so berserk? I can't stress enough how different that behavior was to anything we had ever seen from him. It was pretty much the equivalent of having watched someone you know like the back of your hand suddenly seem very unfamiliar; like you barely know them. If Oliver hadn't been neutered a long time before then, I might've suspected that he had picked up on the scent of a potential mate. Still, that wouldn't have at all explained the strange sensation I felt right after I closed the patio door. But the reality was that I had a lot on my plate; it felt foolish to get so hung up on something that still could've been caused by my imagination.

The following day, things felt like they were mostly back to normal. Oliver trotted outside as soon as I opened the door and did his business without hesitation. Since nobody else in my household seemed too concerned by the racquet during the previous night, it wasn't too hard for me to disregard the feeling that I was being watched.

After a few weeks of typical living, Danny, my youngest boy, started shouting about how he saw a wolf run across the backyard. His story sounded believable until he stated that the animal was moving on two legs like a human. Although Katie and I believed Danny had spotted something, we made the mistake of assuming that he was exaggerating or had misperceived whatever the thing was. In any case, I didn't suspect it was the same animal that had made Oliver go crazy weeks earlier since I thought he would've picked up on its scent. He hadn't seemed to have noticed anything out of the ordinary during that particular occasion. Unfortunately, Danny's sighting freaked him out pretty bad, and he insisted on sleeping on the floor in our bedroom for what was probably at least a week.

But the major horror didn't begin until I received a disturbing phone call from my wife while I was working late one night at the pub. Right away, it was apparent that she had been crying.

"Katie, what's wrong?" I said, anticipating that she was about to inform me that a relative had passed away.

"It's...it's Oliver," she managed to say between sobs. "He's dying."

"What? What do you mean he's dying? What happened?" I said as I walked toward a more private area in the restaurant. I began to hear the sounds of my kids crying in the background.

"Something attacked him," Katie said. "Can you just come home?"

"I'm on my way," I said.

That drive home felt like one of the longest of my life. All of this happened well over twenty years ago, which was before nearly everyone had a cellphone. I so badly yearned for a way to stay in touch with my wife before I could get there. So many awful thoughts had infiltrated my mind; I couldn't help but imagine some of the worst scenarios. Was Oliver already dead? What if whatever attacked him had found a way into our house and harmed Katie and the kids?

I switched on the bright headlights as I neared our driveway, looking carefully at the surrounding woods for any movement, but there was nothing. I made sure to close the garage door before I even opened my car door, and keep in mind this is before I even knew anything about what we were dealing with.

Contrary to what I expected, everything was eerily quiet when I walked inside the house. As I walked toward the kitchen, the first thing I saw was the lump on the floor, covered by a multitude of towels. I didn't need to ask my wife, who I spotted standing near the kitchen sink, what was underneath stacked cloths.

"Are the kids alright?" I said.

"They're fine," Katie said. "I asked them to stay in their rooms until after you arrived home. Her gaze remained on the window near the sink. The back patio lights were on, and it seemed she anticipated something to appear somewhere in the backyard. Even though the situation was grim, I can't begin to tell you how relieved I was to find out that at least my wife and kids were unharmed.

Without saying anything more, I walked over to get a closer look at the one family member who didn't make it. When I lifted a few of the towels, I couldn't believe what I saw. It looked as though a long strip of Oliver's skin had been scraped cleanly from his body, starting from his forehead and going all the way to his rear end, where his tail was missing.

"Did...you see who did this?" I finally managed to mutter while hypnotized by the horror.

"No, but I know it was some kind of large animal," Katie said. "I was shouting for Oliver to get back inside after I heard him aggressively barking and growling. He ignored me, though; something out in those woods had his full attention. Barefoot, I began running in his direction as soon as I heard him yelp. I could tell that he was outmatched by whatever had his attention, and he needed my help. It was before I even made it to the forest edge that I spotted him hobbling toward me. I couldn't help but scream when I saw that a large part of his back was missing, and that was when the kids came running over to the door to check things out. I told them to go away as I tried to rush Oliver inside, but I was so distracted by the sense that he was already dying."

"I'm sorry," I said to my wife while I continued examining my deceased companion. "I should've been here." My intentions for relocating were as genuine as could be. I wanted our family to experience life in a more enriching environment and for me to have a constructive project, but I began to recognize how that project was taking up so much more of my time than I had hoped. I can't begin to imagine how I would've felt had I returned home to find that all of my loved ones had been slaughtered by whatever got the best of Oliver. I knew I had to find a way to kill whatever was out there, or I had to get us out of the area.

I have trouble recalling exactly which stage of our discussion it occurred, but we were interrupted by what I can only describe as a menacing howl. For some reason, I just knew that this long, deep noise was a declaration of domination. There was something about that howl that stated one of us would be next.

"Mom, Mom! I see it!" one of our other sons, Cody, called out from upstairs. "It's behind the woodpile!"

Bear in mind his tone was not one of excitement; it was a tone of immense fear. He was afraid that whatever he spotted was sneaking around and planning its approach toward our house. My other boys immediately started crying after Cody shared his sighting with the household. Since I had an obstructed view of the woodpile from the first floor, I rushed up the steps to see if I could finally get a look at the thing that had made our new life go sour.

"It just ran off," Cody muttered when I made it up to his bedroom. "It went back into the woods. Maybe it heard me yelling about how I saw it."

"What did the animal look like?" I said.

"It was big and grey," Cody said, seemingly shocked and in disbelief of what he saw. Even though it all sounded so crazy, I knew there had to be something to all of it; Cody is my one son who has always been the furthest thing from a practical jokester. Instead, he has always been very well-behaved and mature for his age.

54

I stayed awake for the remainder of the night. With the lights off, I sat by that patio door, awaiting something to stroll through that backyard. Then, finally, there came the point where I noticed what looked like a very tall man standing in the backyard. I assume I dozed off for a second because it felt like the tall figure appeared entirely out of nowhere and happened to be staring directly at my house.

Because it was so dark out, there was only the faintest silhouette of the entity, but believe me, it was out there. It began a slow approach toward the house, seemingly for where I was sitting. Soon, I noticed what was unmistakably a protruding snout and a pair of erect and pointy ears. I then totally understood why my kids claimed the thing could be a werewolf. The sheer size of this thing alone was enough to make me comprehend how it killed my dog so easily.

At that strange moment, I wasn't sure whether I should run outside and try to scare it away or notify my family of a potential ambush. Because the entity wasn't moving toward me at a rapid speed, part of me wanted to wait to find out if we even were an intended target. But, on the other hand, it wouldn't have been the most brilliant move to tangle with this thing if unnecessary. I wasn't even sure whether it was looking at me; it was just too dark to tell.

Reminding myself of what had happened to my canine companion, I would've done anything for the ability to blow the strange creature away. If only I owned a heavy-duty firearm, that creature would've been in pieces scattered all over the lawn.

Slowly, I grabbed hold of the baseball bat that I had leaned against the wall near the doorway. I wanted to be as ready as possible had the wolf-like creature suddenly decided to charge my house, though I had pretty much lost all confidence that a bat would do much of anything against something of that size.

Suddenly, I decided the safest course of action would be to call the police. But when the 9-1-1 dispatcher answered the call, I couldn't think of how to word what was going on other than to state that someone was currently trespassing in my backyard. They agreed to send someone over immediately, and it was as soon as I hung up the phone that I began to worry about what I had just done. What if I was merely welcoming some innocent nightshift police officer to his doom? I debated whether I should call back and tell them that there was a dangerous animal outside my house, but I thought it would sound weird if I were inconsistent.

By the time I crept back over to the window, the wolf-like entity was no longer in sight. I ended up meeting the police officer out front before he could ring the doorbell. I decided it was best not to alert my family that I was worried enough to call the authorities. I thought it might be better if the kids could somehow avoid knowing about that aspect. The officer immediately came off as an approachable guy, so I explained how I wasn't sure about who or what I had seen in the backyard, but I told him how it killed our dog and that multiple other family members had seen it too. When I showed him Oliver's mangled corpse, he gave in to the possibility that there was a fierce predator around our property. That was when he revealed to me that there had been several other mysterious circumstances throughout the area, and it was a bit of an ongoing mystery among the police station. But it was something that he claimed no one had even come close to deciphering.

Even though the officer didn't have his pistol drawn, he kept a hand on it while searching the surrounding wood line. I don't know if it was because I had an armed comrade by my side, but I felt a hell of a lot less tense by that point. Nowadays, I can't help but wonder if that's because the predator was long gone by then. We eventually called it quits, and the officer gave his condolences regarding Oliver one more time before he took off. He said to call back right away if the animal were to return.

My wife and I had a long talk that night, and she was very insistent that she no longer felt safe there. It was clear that she was even more intimidated by the situation than I was, and we ended up renting the place out at a very low rate. We leased a condo that was within walking distance to my pub. The area was a lot more populated, and it was instantly noticeable how much safer that made my family feel. And it made me feel a hell of a lot better when I was working those late nights.

We never again heard anything in the area about the wolf-like creature, not even from the people who rented our property before we sold it a year later. I believe that what we encountered is what is known by many as the *Ozark Howler.*

More Free Books at My Digital Store

If you're looking for NEW reads, check out my digital store www.TomLyonsBooks.com.

Buying my books directly from me means you save money—because my store will always sell for less than big retailers. My store also offers sales, deals, bundles, and pre-order discounts you won't find anywhere else.

Visit my store now to check out exclusive books and other products not available anywhere else!

Report #3

Hey there, my name is Cameron, and although I'm not at liberty to identify which news network I worked for, our base camp was visited by quite the strange entities while I was on an assignment in the Middle East. Our camp was attacked, and it's something I still have trouble accepting as reality.

In 2004, the network sent us to Afghanistan on a relatively simple assignment. Our job was to interview various locals on how they felt about their interactions with the US troops. I believe we were assigned to be there for about two weeks to acquire a reasonable number of contrasting opinions. We traveled around the regions that were currently occupied by US forces, and it was only the third or fourth night we were there that we encountered something that my mind can't make any sense of.

I remember there was a bad dust storm around 8:00 or 9:00 PM. The news crew and I were inside our assigned housing unit, planning for the next day's schedule, when we heard shouting followed by gunfire. Even though it was alarming, we were taught to mentally prepare ourselves for that sort of thing due to the occasional rebel attack. However, it wasn't all that long before something entirely out of the ordinary occurred.

We heard what sounded like a heavy object landing atop the roof of another nearby housing unit. When one of our crew members cracked the door open, I heard him gasp.

"What the hell?" he said while looking upward. I had no idea what he could be looking at; after all, there was no noise from helicopters or other aircraft. And this occurred well before any of the opposition were equipped with drones.

"What? What is it?" one of the other crewmembers said.

"I could've sworn I just saw a couple of men in gliders fly by from above," he said. The tone of his voice conveyed that he was as confused as ever. Just then, we heard another one of those same crashes; a scream and more gunfire followed. Alarms sounded, and we were soon instructed to lock the door and remain inside the facility.

Sporadic gunfire continued for the next five minutes, but it wasn't until the next day that our crew received a better idea of what had happened. Allegedly, a group of large, winged creatures resembling bats ambushed a group of soldiers and harassed them on their way back to camp. And it turned out that the loud thud we heard near our housing unit came from a soldier getting picked up and dropped onto the roof of another housing unit. Fortunately, that guy survived with just a few puncture wounds and broken bones. The journalist I was working with tried to interview that man or anyone else who was in combat with these alleged winged beasts, but the military denied the request.

I spent the rest of our time in Afghanistan, wondering whether the creatures would show up again. I wasn't sure what to believe, but whatever had happened, it was clear that the military didn't want word of it getting out. Ever since that day, I've become obsessed with reading about cryptids in my spare time.

Report #4

Back when my grandparents were still alive, they lived in a town called Fort Wayne, Indiana. I loved visiting them because my grandmother was a spectacular cook, and my grandfather was an avid outdoorsman. That worked out rather well for my mother, who was single and worked long hours as a nurse. Some of my fondest childhood memories come from my time spent with them. But there was one occasion where I experienced such intense fear that I struggled with being anywhere near natural bodies of water for a couple of years after.

Fishing was one of my favorite things to do with my grandpa. I loved listening to stories from his past while he puffed on a cigar. He always smoked a cigar while we fished off his modest-sized motorboat. He was that guy who regularly wore the vest full of various small lures, but I don't think I ever saw him bait his hooks with anything other than nightcrawlers. I suppose he liked to feel stylish while out on the water.

My frightening experience happened over thirty years ago, so you'll have to forgive me that I'm not 100% sure which lake we were on at the time, but after doing some internet research, I want to say it was one called Crooked Lake. There's a chain of lakes in that area, and we had probably visited every one of them throughout my childhood summers. I would've thought that the event's venue would've remained more prominent in my memory, but it's just the event itself that has held all clarity. I even remember how my grandpa told me a story about his time in the Navy right before the whole thing occurred.

We had drifted near the shore, where there happened to be a doe and a couple of fawns hydrating. They didn't seem too worried about us coming close to them since they were probably used to fishermen. It had to be the loudest splash I've ever heard when the enormous, armored animal lunged out from underneath the water and snatched one of the fawns with what looked to be a razor-sharp beak. It had to be the most explosive, startling thing I've ever witnessed. This thing looked like a snapping turtle, but it was so large that my grandpa could've easily convinced me it was a dinosaur. We couldn't see the whole animal, but it was a charcoal grey color, and its skin had a rigid, scaly texture.

The doe and the other fawn ran for cover as the little one got thrashed around near the shore. That only lasted a few seconds before the turtle-like beast turned and bolted beneath the surface with its prey still in its beak. The commotion disturbed the water's surface so immensely that Grandpa almost fell from his seat. It was so much like what we see in nature documentaries when a crocodile snatches a wildebeest from a river shore. The level of natural power this prehistoric-looking animal had was staggering.

Stunned, my grandpa and I continued to observe as the fawn struggled near the water surface. The whole thing happened so close to us that one of the mammal's hooves smacked the side of our boat while getting dragged into deeper water. Soon, both animals were nowhere to be found. When I think about it now, I suspect the turtle-like predator had only brought its prey into deeper water to ensure that it drowned. Although we never saw them reemerge, I bet the predator had a feeding ground or a nest within a nearby marsh that wasn't visible to us. The ambush occurred with such lightning speed that we never would've noticed anything had we not been so close to the action.

My grandpa wanted to ride his boat around to search for the unidentified beast, but he soon realized how freaked out I was. I remember thinking that that animal for sure possessed enough power to tip the small boat and that it probably would've had we gotten too close to its nest. After seeing how shaken up I was, he decided to call it quits for the day.

After we finally pulled the boat from the water and got inside my grandpa's truck, I felt a lot better. Suddenly, the encounter had become so much easier for me to talk about. Unfortunately for her, my grandma spent the next few hours having to repeatedly hear about how her grandson had seen a "water dinosaur" catch and eat a baby deer. Fortunately, my grandpa was there to back up the story, though he didn't see it like we had encountered a dinosaur, but rather the country's most overgrown snapping turtle. Nevertheless, I was so thrilled about the sighting, even though I never again agreed to explore that chain of lakes.

Years later, I learned that there's a legend regarding an enormous turtle-like creature within the state of Indiana; go figure! It's known as the *Beast of Busco*, having happened in the town of Churubusco. The first recorded sighting occurred all the way back in 1898. The next reported encounter took place in the summer of 1948. Both sightings happened in a body of water known as Fulk Lake. The reports match what my grandpa and I saw, claiming to have spotted a giant snapping turtle that weighed an estimated 500 pounds.

Since turtles are known to be one of the longest-living species on the planet, I wonder if we might've encountered the same organism from those earlier sightings. Nowadays, I feel so fortunate to have stumbled upon something so scarce. Without a doubt, that whole experience made me into more of an open-minded individual.

If you ever find yourself at a body of water near Fort Wayne, Indiana, be sure to keep an eye out.

Are you enjoying the read?

I have decided to give back to the readers by making the following eBook **FREE!**

To claim your free eBook, head over to

www.LivingAmongBigfoot.com

and click the "FREE BOOK" tab!

Report #5

My name is Hank, and I'd like to start off by expressing my appreciation that you took the time to read this. Nearly a decade has passed since this eerie period in my family's life, and it was what sparked enough motivation for me to finally move out of the town I had grown up in.

I was born and raised in the remarkably quaint town of Laurel, Delaware. Even if you've ever lived in the northeastern part of the country, there's still a pretty darn good chance you've never heard of the place. In my opinion, it's a charming place to visit, but with only 4,000 residents, it stays under the radar.

I was 25 years old when my best friend, Sharon, and I, decided to settle down and start a family. We were never very romantic or anything, but neither of us found dating other people very fruitful. Since we got along so well, we concluded that we'd be a good match for raising children together. That might sound strange to some people, but Sharon and I had known each other since we were little kids, so we were very comfortable discussing anything.

When our little girl, Jessica, was born less than a year after getting married, we knew we made the right decisions. However, it was right around Jessica's fourth birthday that strange circumstances began to arise. Although I'm not certain, I think the experiences had a lot to do with the house we moved into around that time. But the main reason I'm not sure is that the structure didn't have too long of a history, and I've always been under the impression that there's supposed to be a correlation with that.

Maybe a year or so after Jessica's birth, we received news from a doctor that Sharon had lost the ability to have more children, so Jessica remained a single child.

I believe the first peculiar incident was when Sharon and I were in the kitchen and heard what sounded like a ball bouncing back and forth above us. Immediately, the situation was odd because Jessica was much more the type to want to spend her time working on art than playing with a ball. We were comfortable leaving her alone in her room ever since she was very young because she almost always worked on coloring books or drew on blank paper. Jessica's bedroom was directly above the kitchen, and the flooring was made of beautiful hardwood. My wife and I were very keen on keeping the house in tiptop shape, so I walked over to the stairway and called out to my daughter to not bounce any objects while in her bedroom. She didn't respond, but the noise immediately stopped; however, the annoying noise resumed a few minutes later. That time, Sharon walked up the steps to talk with Jessica.

"Okay, Mommy," I could hear Jessica responding before my wife could make her way to the top of the staircase. We were both back in the kitchen carrying on with making dinner when yet again, the bouncing noise returned. By this point, I had heard the noise enough to observe that it didn't sound like just one person playing with a ball. As crazy as it sounded, I could've sworn that I heard the object getting bounced from one end of the room to the other; then, there would be a slight pause before a nearly identical pace went back across the room. I carefully listened to the repeating pattern, requiring an increasing amount of effort to convince myself I wasn't losing my mind.

"Did you hear someone else up there?" I said to Sharon.

She glanced at me like she must have misunderstood what I had asked. "What are you talking about?"

"Listen," I said. "Is it me, or does it sound like Jessica's bouncing the ball up there?"

We both stopped what we were doing and stayed quiet for a few seconds. Although she still thought the idea was crazy, Sharon seemed to get where I was coming from. She walked back up the stairs, and I heard the bouncing stop right before she entered my daughter's bedroom. Since everything remained calm, I got back to whatever I was tending to in the kitchen.

"All good?" I said as Sharon arrived back at my side.

"I suppose so," she said.

"What do you mean?"

"Well—" Sharon hesitated, "she claimed she was bouncing the rubber ball with a friend by the name of Thomas, but, of course, there was no one else in her bedroom. I couldn't tell if Jessica was trying to be serious or not. Maybe she's gotten to an age where she's going to want to play practical jokes on us."

"Maybe," I muttered. But something seemed off.

Throughout the years, there was a variety of happenings that just didn't make sense. Both Sharon and I felt like we were tricking ourselves. There were times where it almost felt like I was in some video game world with regular-occurring glitches. There were even a few times where I noticed objects levitating an inch or two from the surfaces beneath them. But nothing compared to what happened one autumn night.

My wife and I were sharing a bottle of wine downstairs when we heard Jessica run out of her bedroom, down the hallway. That wasn't like her. But the disturbing part was when we heard the second pair of much heavier footsteps charging after her around five seconds later.

"Jessica!" I shouted just as my wife lost grip on her wineglass, which shattered upon the kitchen floor. I was the first one up the steps and fully prepared to confront any sick pervert who had decided to break into our home and terrorize my little girl. But it soon became apparent that my panicked wife and I were now the only ones creating any commotion; everything else had gone so eerily silent.

"Jessica?" I shouted again, but there was no response. Due to the direction that we heard Jessica running, she could've entered only one of two rooms, and both doors were shut. Since our daughter wasn't giving us any indication regarding which room she had entered, I chose the nearest door, which led to the guestroom. There was nobody in there, and the space appeared untouched, but it was an entirely different story when we entered our bedroom.

Nearly every object in our room was on the floor. Every book, every mirror, every piece of furniture were scattered about. How did all of that happen within the minuscule amount of time it took us to get up there? Maybe it was because our adrenaline had taken over, but neither of us had heard these items spilling onto the floor; that makes absolutely no sense. The only thing in our bedroom to even remotely suppress the noise of spilling objects was a thin rug covering only a fraction of the hardwood floor. But, of course, I disregarded that mystery in the heat of the moment to focus on defending my little girl.

"What are you doing under there?" Sharon said after peeking beneath our bed. Her tone conveyed that Jessica was tucked under there alone and likely unharmed, so I continued searching throughout our bedroom and private bathroom.

"Shh!" Jessica said, "you're going to ruin our game!"

"What game?" Sharon said.

"We're playing hide and seek!" Jessica whispered, insinuating that we were ruining the fun.

"Who are you playing with?" Sharon said, determined to establish that our daughter was alone, and we had merely fooled ourselves. Had we somehow misinterpreted that there was a second set of footsteps?

"I heard Thomas go into your closet when he heard you guys coming up the stairs," Jessica said. There was no sign of trepidation in her voice.

Whatever was going on in her world, she seemed to think it was completely normal. Just then, I thought I heard a bit of ruffling coming from inside our walk-in closet. The light was off when I tore the door open, but I could've sworn I saw what looked like a pair of old moccasins or some other type of outdated footwear protruding beneath my shirt rack.

The reason I noticed them right away is that they weren't at all familiar. The only reason I felt a little more at ease was that the shoes appeared child-sized. Therefore, I didn't feel as threatened as I would've if it had been an adult who somehow snuck into our home. In any case, it was as soon as I flipped the light switch that the odd-looking footwear vanished. I aggressively checked in every little crevice where someone could've been hiding, but there was no one.

"There's nobody else here," I stated as I shut off the light and closed the closet door behind me.

"That's because you scared him off!" Jessica argued as she crawled her way out from under our bed.

"Sweety, why did you mess up our room like this?" Sharon said, still kneeling beside our bed.

"It wasn't me, Mommy; it was Thomas," Jessica replied.

"Thomas isn't able to touch things in this world," my wife said, at least playing along with the idea that Thomas was more than an imaginary friend. We had found it a bit troublesome to talk to our daughter about our assumed reality that Thomas didn't exist, the reason being that Jessica was a bit socially awkward since she was a child. Even when we had family friends over, the children would play with Jessica for a little bit and then seemed to wander off in search of other entertainment. We had yet to establish whether our daughter wasn't interested in socializing or if the other kids were shy, but she just hadn't yet had much luck making friends. The supposed imagination of Thomas seemed to keep her occupied, so we decided to let it be and assume that she'd eventually grow out of it.

The next alarming incident occurred one evening before I had returned home from work. My wife told me that she was looking everywhere for our daughter, but she wasn't responding. She assumed she must've been entertaining herself with another game of *Hide and Seek*, so she went to check under our bed. Although Jessica wasn't there, Sharon's heart nearly skipped a beat when she spotted the old-looking moccasins atop the floor on the other side of the bed. She claimed she could see stumpy, hair legs protruding out of them, making it very clear that it was anyone other than our daughter standing mere feet away from her. In addition to that, she said it looked like there was dark hair plopped on the floor just behind the shoes. She only glimpsed it before she sprang to her feet, but then there wasn't anyone or anything in sight. In a state of disbelief, she jogged to the other side of the bed and did the same routine of checking underneath. Again, there was nothing. Eventually, Sharon found our daughter down in our dusty basement, claiming that she *was* playing another game of *Hide and Seek* with Thomas, but this time, she didn't want to be found because Thomas was in a bad mood.

Later that night, my wife and I were lying in bed, quietly discussing our daughter's mental health, when our closet door suddenly burst open. Now, this is where things get really damn weird. I don't know if something teleported us or if we were somehow wiped of our memories from during that brief period, but my wife and I found ourselves tied to a couple of the larger trees in our backyard. Although there wasn't anything covering our mouths, neither of us could speak. We wanted to yell out to get anyone's attention, but it was impossible. It felt like my jaw muscles were paralyzed.

Suddenly, Jessica walked into view. She was still wearing her pajamas, and fortunately, appeared unharmed. But it was easy to tell that her spirits were low like she maybe felt sad or guilty. I badly wanted to command her to run, but no matter how hard I tried, I couldn't.

"Thomas brought you both here because he's upset," Jessica said. "But he says he won't hurt either of you...or me...if he receives an apology for disrespecting him."

It was then that I heard footsteps and a few raspy breaths emanating from behind Sharon and me. Again, I wanted to yell for my daughter to run, but it was no use. Jessica seemed relatively unphased by whoever or whatever was with us. I got the impression that she knew this sort of thing was coming, but she didn't know how to warn us.

"He's going to let you speak now," Jessica said, "but I'm supposed to let you know that if you do anything other than what Thomas is asking, he's going to kill me in front of you." That was the moment when our daughter lost her composure, and she started tearing up. "Thomas said he's going to stop you from breathing for a few moments, just so you know he's serious," Jessica reluctantly added only seconds before my lungs felt like they were underwater.

"Please, Thomas, stop it! You're scaring us!" Jessica cried out to whatever entity we still couldn't see. It was apparent that my daughter had been instructed to keep the volume of her voice to a minimum. I had begun to feel like I was about to lose consciousness just before I was able to breathe again via my nostrils. Moments later, my daughter started to levitate maybe half a foot from the ground, and I could tell that she was experiencing a similar paralysis. The terrified look in her eyes conveyed that she wanted to scream for help, but it was impossible. Right then, I could feel my jaw muscles begin to function again, and the only thing I could think to blurt out was, "I'm sorry! Let Jessica go! Please! I'm so sorry!"

It felt like I blinked before my wife and I woke up in our bed. Everything in our room was nice and tidy, but our panicked states helped confirm that what just happened was anything but imaginary. Without sharing a word, we simultaneously jumped out of bed and shouted our daughter's name. After bursting into her bedroom, we found her lying in bed, awake and lacking energy, but, fortunately, unharmed.

We never spent another night in that house, and I drove us to a highway motel in one of the other nearest towns. Alone, I went back home on several occasions to pack stuff up without ever being bothered. Jessica never claimed to see Thomas again, so I can't help but think that, for whatever reason, he decided to separate himself from our lives.

Since we believe our daughter faced significant trauma from her interactions with the entity, Sharon and

I have always limited the amount we discuss the subject. However, a therapist asked Jessica to draw Thomas around a year after the events took place, and she shared the illustration with Sharon and me in private. It would be an understatement to say that the sketch was unsettling.

Jessica first sketched herself, and then she drew her interpretation of Thomas standing next to her. To me, he very much looked like a character from a fairytale. He was about the same height as my daughter, and his clothes looked as though they were from the Middle Ages. This lifeform wasn't human. The best way I can describe it is that it looked like a troll with very pointy ears, all-white eyes, and long black hair that went all the way to its feet. A chill made its way down my spine as I noticed the figure wore moccasin-like shoes that were very similar to what I thought I saw in our dark closet that one strange night. And Sharon confirmed that they accurately portrayed what she spotted on the floor near the other side of our bed.

Of course, we have no way of verifying what we encountered, but both Sharon and I suspect we were visited by a cryptid known as the *pukwudgie*. According to the therapist, Jessica doesn't know why Thomas was so upset with my wife and me. For whatever reason, the entity didn't share this information with our daughter. The only semi-logical theory we've been able to come to is that the entity heard Sharon and me discussing how we assumed he wasn't real and that that deeply insulted him. But if that was the case, why didn't he reveal himself to us and leave our child out of it?

One thing is clear: we live in a damn strange world.

Conclusion

Thanks for reading! Be sure to check out *Stay Out of the Woods: Strange Encounters, Volume 3!*

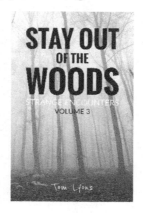

Editor's Note

Before you go, I'd very much like to say "thank you" for purchasing this book.

I'm aware you had an endless variety of cryptid-related books to choose from, but you took a chance on my content. Therefore, thanks for reading this one and sticking with it to the last page.

At this point, I'd like to ask you for a *tiny* favor; it would mean the world to me if you could submit a review where you purchased it.

Your feedback will aid me as I continue to create products that you and many others can enjoy.

Mailing List Sign Up Form

Don't forget to sign up for the newsletter email list. I promise this will not be used to spam you, but only to ensure that you will always receive the first word on any new releases, discounts, or giveaways! All you need to do is visit the following URL and enter your email address.

URL-

http://eepurl.com/dhnspT

Social Media

Feel free to follow/reach out to me with any questions or concerns on either Instagram or Twitter! I will do my best to follow back and respond to all comments.

Instagram:

@living_among_bigfoot

Twitter:

@AmongBigfoot

About the Editor

A simple man at heart, Tom Lyons lived an ordinary existence for his first 52 years. Native to the great state of Wisconsin, he went through the motions of everyday life, residing near his family and developing a successful online business. The world that he once knew would completely change shortly after moving out west, where he was confronted by the allegedly mythical species known as Bigfoot.

You can email him directly at:

Living.Among.Bigfoot@gmail.com

Made in the USA
Monee, IL
30 September 2024

66840316R00073